T0381361

Keep on Rejoicing

Carolyn M.G. Fletcher

AuthorHouse™
1663 Liberty Drive
Bloomington, IN 47403
www.authorhouse.com
Phone: 1 (800) 839-8640

Published by AuthorHouse 05/31/2019

ISBN: 978-1-7283-0982-8 (sc)
ISBN: 978-1-7283-0981-1 (e)

Library of Congress Control Number: 2019905199

Print information available on the last page.

Scripture taken from The Holy Bible, King James Version. Public Domain

This book is printed on acid-free paper.

authorHOUSE®

Contents

Be Happy

Happiness is found along the way . . .
Not at the end of the road.

"For thou shalt eat the labour of thine hands;happy shalt thou be, and it shall be well with thee."

Psalms 128:2

Saved
When God saves you
Give thanks back to him: you're blessed
So, give what's due

Being Small is Beautiful

As we journey and walk these dangerous roads of life
We see God's beauty everywhere.

Each day when we awake, we should say to God
Good morning and thank you for another beautiful day.
Then say to yourself; I am beautiful and wonderfully made by God.

Take the little you have and put him first and he'll multiply it for you
For he make small things become big.

To serve him from a heart of love, that's all he asks of you. When you put him first.
We may not do anything big in life but, being small is beautiful.

*"He hath made every thing beautifyl in his time : also he hath set the
world in their heart so that no man can find out the work that God
maketh from the beginning to the end." (Ecclesiastes 3:11)*

He's Not Dead

Christ suffered high upon the cross
To save sinners who are lost.
Upon his head a thorny crown, he wore
To suffer all sin and shame.
It hurt him, but he didn't frown
He hung there and the blood came streaming down
Now what have we to offer thee
For he paid it all for you and me.
For he's not dead can't you see
He now lives within me.

"I am he that liveth, and was dead; and, behold I am alive for evermore, Amen; and have the keys of hell and death." (Revelation 1:18)

What God is Like to Me

He's like a pair of shoes . . .
    walks with you every step of the way.
He's like scotch tape . . .
    you can't see him, but you know he's there. . .
He's like the air we breathe . . .
    you need him to survive
He's like cool water . . .
    quenches your every thirst
He's like a light . . .
    shining through the darkness
He's like a rope. . .
    gives you strength to hold on
He's like a well . . . .
    It's never empty
He's like a clock . . . .
    Always on time

"The Lord is my light and my salvation; whom shall I fear?
The Lord is the strength of my life; of whom shall I be afraid?" (Psalms 27:1)

"God is a Spirit: and they that worship him must worship him in spirit and truth."
(John 4:24)

Trusting God with My Life

Lord it's a blessing to trust you with my life.

I put it in your hands to carry me through each task that I face.

Thank you, for your blessings are new each morning.

You cause the sun to set, and the rain to fall.

You bless man to bring forth food out of the earth to feed his family.

You bless us with water to drink and to quench our thirst.

We're blessed to have jobs and warm beds to sleep in, and clothes on our backs.

I serve a wonderful God for when the praises go up, God's blessings come down.

"Bless the LORD, O my soul; and all that is within me, bless His holy name!
Bless the LORD, O my soul, and forget not all His benefits:" (Psalm 10:3-1-2)

"Trust in the LORD, and do good; so shalt thou dwell in the land, and verily thou shalt be fed.
Delight thyself also in the LORD: and he shall give thee the desires of thine heart."

(Psalm 37:3-4)

Open My Eyes

Thank you, Lord, for this beautiful
spring day to be awakened by your touch.
To see the sun shining,
and to hear the birds singing their song.
Your deep desires of nature
bless the withered flowers with
new life, as the budding earth flourishes again.
My soul opens to your touch, and I am renewed.
Lord, I believe your promises and that you have marvelous plans for my life.
A plan that's more than I could ever imagine. My hope and future lives in you.
Order my steps and lead me to do your perfect will.

"But thanks to be to God, which giveth us the victory through our Lord Jesus Christ."
(1 Corinthians 15:57)

"Giving thanks always for all things unto God and the Father in
the name of our Lord Jesus Christ;" (Ephesians 5:20)

Blessings Come When the Dark Shadows Fall

When trouble comes, and things go wrong,
knowing that sickness and sorrows come to us all.
Your days are cheerless, and the nights are long,
Remember that God is still there, so sing him a song.
He'll comfort your heart and give you peace of mind.
For no man can grow without struggle or strife, the more we endure,
we'll have patience and grace, so stay in line and run the race.
Look for a rainbow in the sky and God will wipe tears from your eyes.

"I will make them and the places all around my hill a blessing; and I will cause showers to come down in his season; there shall be showers of blessing." (Ezekiel 34:26)

Stand Still and Wait

Whatever you're going through hold on to God's unchanging hand.
He'll take care of you, he's faithful to what he started in you so stand still and "listen."
God will calm your fears, so allow yourself to be covered fully by his blood.
Let Go and Let God.
Just say yes to his will, he'll keep you on track so just live for him.
Stand still and wait on God.
Being confident of this very thing;
That he who hath begun a good work
In you will perform it until the day of Jesus Christ.

'Being confident of this very thing, that he which hath begun a good work in you will perform it until the day of Jesus Christ:" (Philippians 1:6)

Quietness of The Night

Just knowing how things are still
in the quietness of the night.
The birds have stopped their singing
The stars are shining bright
You can sit and talk to God
In the quietness of the night.
Peace of mind is what you'll have
When all the house is still.
God will answer your every prayer
So, concentrate to do his will

*" I must work the works of him that sent me, while it is day: the
night cometh, when no man can work," (John 9:4)*

*"Be still and know that I am God; I will be exalted among the
heathen, I will be exalted in the earth!" (Psalm 46:10)*

Recipe of Faith

4 Eggs for Obedience – Brings Blessings
1 Cup of Butter for - Endurance and Strong Faith
2 ½ Cups of Milk for – Patience – his perfect works
2 Cups of Sugar for Wisdom – Gives Understanding

Pour into a large bowl
Blend all ingredients together
Pour into Baking Pan
Cover Until Well Done

Serve with strong faith, prayer and understanding.

The grass withers
The flowers fade
But God's word stands forever.

Isaiah: 40:8–––

God Is Love

Thought:
God will keep you,
If you want to be kept.

When I Am Gone

As I walk this road of life
I've had many trials to face
I struggle so hard with many of them
going through on God's Grace.
The pain and struggle, sorrow,
stress and grief. God has taken me
Through it all, in him I do believe
I know that there's a brighter side
That, I've been told.
For I only live here one time
On earth before reaching my final home.
So, when I'm gone, don't cry for me.
I'll be on the other side, where
Life is free from the cares of this world.
Now that I'm free, no pain, no suffering
no bills to pay. So, don't try to reach me by cellphone
for there's none up there.
So, keep on looking upward and we'll see one another
face-to-face again in the city far away.

"All we like sheep have gone astray;
We have turned, everyone, to his own way;
And the LORD hath laid on Him the iniquity of us all." (Isaiah 53:6)

"Because He Lives, We Too Shall Live"

In this restless world of struggle, it's very hard to find
Answers to the questions that come daily to our minds
We cannot see the future, what's beyond is still unknown
For the secret of God's kingdom still belongs to him alone.

But he granted us salvation, when his son was crucified
For life became immortal, because our savior died.
And to know life is unending and God's love is endless too,
Makes each daily task we face, much easier to do.

For our Savior's Resurrection, was God's way of telling men,
That in Christ we are eternal, and in him we live again.

*"I am he that liveth, and was dead; and, behold, I am alive for evermore,
Amen; and have the keys of hell and of death." (Revelation 1:18)*

Be Not Afraid

God answers our prayers when we're obedient to him and do his will.
Hope along with faith causes us to receive from God.
We live in the elements of his love.
He makes our enemies our footstool.
Put him first in everything that you do, and be not afraid
In all thy ways acknowledge him, and
He shall direct they path.
Loving God is the best thing that you can do,
so, fear not what man can do to you.
Make the most of your time serving God and be not afraid.
Walk in wisdom, put God first,
your reward is at the end of the race.
For God hath not given us the spirit of fear; but of power, and of love, and of a sound mind.
So Be Not Afraid

"For God hath not given us a spirit of fear, but of power and of love and of a sound mind." (II Timothy 1:7)

God is So Wonderful Because

A – He's Awesome	N – He's a Nurturing God
B – He's Blameless	O – He's the Omnipotent
C – He's Our Creator	P – He's Our Protector
D – He's Our Deliverer	Q – He's Quiet and Quick
E – He's the Everlasting God	R – He's the Rock, Rescuer and Rewarder
F – He's Our Father	S – He's Our Savior, Shephard and Shield
G – He's a Great God	T – He's a Teacher
H – He's a Healer	U – He's Unsearchable and Unlimited
I – He's Our Instructor	V – He's a Victorious God
J – He's Our Judge	W – He's a Wonderful Way maker
K – He's the King of Kings	X – He's like an X-Ray Machine, knows you completely
L – He's the Lord of Lords	Y – He's Yearning for You
M – He's the Most High over all the Earth	Z – He's Zealous

Don't Forget God

All the time you spend outside of God, you lose time.
Come in for everything you have
God gave it to you.
Just think back when you had nothing much
and where he brought you from.
Now you have more than enough, so don't lose out
Sell out to God and be blessed.
Help those less fortunate than you.
Encourage people to pray and step out on his word.
The Lord will give strength unto his people. The Lord will bless his people with peace.
Don't forget God, give him your best.
In all thy ways acknowledge him and he shall direct thy paths.

"In all thy ways acknowledge him, and he shall direct thy paths." (Proverbs 3:6)

Jesus Paid It All

When you count all the cost it takes to follow Jesus
There are no flowery beds of ease
Through suffering and raging battle
And the heat of it all,
still give Glory to his name.
For he never left you alone,
he laid the foundation and opened the way.
So, don't forget where he's brought you from.
You can't forget how much he paid.
So, don't ever let go of his hand, for Jesus paid it all.

"And being in an agony he prayed more earnestly: and his sweat was as it were great drops of blood falling down to the ground." (Luke 22:44)

"For even hereunto were ye called: because Christ also suffered for us, leaving us an example, that ye should follow his steps:" (I Peter 2:21)

It's Everybody's Job

If everybody would tell somebody
About God's amazing grace, there
Would be less confusion among the human race.
If nobody told anybody; then our people will continue to fuss
And fight, and there'll be lots
Of bloodshed, and many tears.
For anybody could start a fight and wind up dead
Now those are lost souls that'll never be fed.
So, come on everybody and help spread
God's word and do his will.
God will fight your battle if you just stand still.

*"Be still, and know that I am God: I will be exalted among the
heathen, I will be exalted in the eath." (Psalm 46:10)*

"If I were hungry, I would not tell thee: for the world is mine, and the fullness thereof."
(Psalm 50:12)

*"If my people , which are called by my name, shall humble themselves, and
pray, and seek my face, and turn from their wicked ways; then will I hear
from heaven, and will forgive their sin, and will heal their land."*
(II Chronicles 7:14)

The Dogwood Tree

Just a little twig
My sister took it from the branch of a dogwood tree
And she explained to me that this is a symbol of the cross
Where Jesus hung with the nail prints in his hand.
Yes, he hung there on the cross for you and me and died,
So that we may live.

"But God forbid that I should glory, save in the cross of our Lord Jesus Christ, by whom the world is crucified unto me, and I unto the world." (Galatians 6:14)

"Looking unto Jesus, the author and finisher of our faith, who for the joy that was set before Him endured the cross, despising the shame, and is sat down at the right hand of the throne of God." (Hebrews 12:2)

A New Day of Blessings

Each morning when you wake to start a new day
Stretch out your arms to God and thank him for the day.
As you kneel down to pray, joy will fill
Your heart knowing that he's with you from the start.
Smile and say how great it is just to still be alive.
Knowing some love one left during the night,
not even saying goodbye.
We must be thankful for we're bought with a price, so think about the joys
You have in life. Living for God is the right thing to do.
He will supply all your needs, and some wants too.
For your blessings are new each day.

"The blessing of the LORD it maketh rich, and he addeth no sorrow with it." (Proverbs 10:22)

Don't Rob the Lord

One morning when I awaken, all in a rush. I cleaned up very quickly and rushed out the door to catch the bus. Forgetting to pray or even talk to the Lord. With my tithes in my pocket I said oh, there's a robber on that bus. As I stepped on the bus and took a seat, this tall slim young man sat next to me. As the door shut, the bus rolled down the street. This same young man started talking to me. As I clutched my purse tightly, I said oh lord, don't let him rob me. My tithes are on board. I planned on spending it on somethings I really need; for I'll catch up on my tithes when I have more indeed.

The bus continued to move on down a steep hill; and came to a rushing stop. Then, that slim young man jumped up and said, "driver don't hit that truck." As the truck slowly moved down the road, I said Lord please take care of all of us today, knowing I hadn't taken time out to pray, or even put my tithes away.

When I arrived at work all cold and wet, there I thanked the Lord for a safe trip. Knowing the robber didn't snatch my purse, as he jumped onto another bus for work. I thanked the Lord again and again for my tithes still in my purse.

I put all my personal belongings away and went up to my floor. There, I got myself together as I did my work. Tithes now safely locked up.

Thinking about Sunday morning for that's my usual day at church, singing and praising the Lord with all the other saints.

When Sunday came around, I was still carrying my tithes in my purse, knowing now I had to go to church. Service was a blessing and I prayed, sang and shouted. I thanked the Lord for keeping me safe. When tithe and offering time came around, and I thought about what I had to do. I passed that plate right by or would you pay your tithes?

When service was over, I started out the door. The sun was shining so bright a big smile covering my face. For I was the robber at that point you see. Leaving the Lord unpaid for blessing me.

"Will a man rob God? Yet ye have robbed Me!
But he say, 'Wherein have we robbed Thee?' In tithes and offerings."
(Malachi 3:8)

"I robbed other churches, taking wages from them to do your service."
(II Corinthians 11:8)

Precious Memories

The Lord blessed me with a wonderful mother who kept me in her care. Taught me right from wrong and gave me tender love and care. But now I'm all grown up and I do things differently now, but I still remember mother's love, for I must go on.

I surprised myself one day and went out for a drive. I stopped by my mother's old house, and, Oh! to my surprise. For I knew she wasn't there, for the Lord had called her home. But the memories of her and that little house still linger on.

So, I stopped just to look around, and I sat down on the steps for a minute or two. I began to praise the Lord and a sweet spirit filled the air. Oh, I thank the Lord for meeting me there, and to my surprise, I found myself on the inside. What happened after that you'll never know.

But when I got myself together, I was ready to go. For outside the grass seemed so green, the flowers in full bloom. The bees were buzzing and the birds humming their tune. For those precious memories of her will still linger on. For she now lives in her brand-new home.

"Blessed are they who keep His testimonies,
and that seek Him with the whole heart!" (Psalm 119:2)

Friends

Friends never question you
You don't have to ask
It shows in what you say and do
No matter what the task.
You cannot see it with your eyes
Or Hold it in your hand
Together we must work and try
To keep God's simple plan.
A man named Jesus shows the way
He teaches us what to do
Love one another everyday
As much as I love you.

When trials and troubles challenge you
And life seems so unfair
Hand in hand, he will see you through.
Together we can hear
Over the years as we grow
We may be put through the test
It's truly up to us you know.
As friends we are the best.

"A friend loveth at all times, and a brother is born for adversity." (Proverbs 17:17)

God Made Me Somebody

I was nobody, but I prayed day and night, asking God to make me alright.

For I know, I have sinned and come short of the glory of God carrying my heavy burdens and bearing my trials.

I tried many times climbing the rough hills, even dragged through the dusty mill, but tears still always run down my face, but I must go on and win the race.

So, I reached out and grabbed a hold of God's hand and headed up the dusty road. I couldn't see just what was ahead, so I told it all to God instead. The road got clearer as I went along, walking with Jesus, feeling no harm. I am not afraid I said with a big smile, because God made me somebody, for, I am his child.

He blessed me right there in the middle of the road, now I can carry the load. For its no secret what God can do, if he blesses me, he'll bless you too.

For I have a great determination to win this race. Yes, God has made me somebody and I feel just great.

"Ye are of God, little children, and have overcome them, because greater is he that is in you than he that is in the world." (I John 4:4)

How Can I Say Goodbye?

How can I say goodbye to you little brother (Cliff)
When our time together seemed so short.
I'll miss you for all the good times we shared
When you were the boss
On those fishing days, sleigh riding, and cutting/chopping wood
In the cold, even putting up the chickens, you kept things in control.
On that last day when I knelt beside your bed,
You held my hand so tightly to keep back the tears.

But in so much pain, you knew the Lord and Savior and called
On his name. The Lord lifted your burdens, now nothing is the same.
(Cliff) there will always be a special place in my heart for you.
So, go on and take your rest. I love you very much,
But God Loves You Best

"By this all men know that ye are my disciples, if ye have love one to another." (John 13:35"

Our Love Shows

To all our children we love so dear,
Ripping and running from here to there.
It's lots of fun when the children are around
They make us smile even when we frown.
We show our love in many ways
To let time, pass on, for pleasant days.
So, without our children the world wouldn't grow
So, we're very proud to let our love show.

"Now ye are clean through the word which I have spoken unto you." (John 15:3)

What Christmas Means to Me

Christmas is a time of giving praises to our Lord and Savior Jesus Christ
Who was born in a stable, on a cold winter's night.
For a star glowed above the stable where the baby Jesus lay,
and even the animals kept silent to give him praise.
For his bed was made of straw and sweet spirits filled the air,
the angels singing so sweetly brought joy to the world.
On this Christmas day, my joy can overflow, knowing the Savior of my life
Is Jesus Christ the Lord

*"Great is the LORD, and greatly to be praised;
And His greatness is unsearchable." (Psalm 145:3)*

"Nurses" Just Whisper A Prayer

You all are just so sweet and kind
so just relax everything is fine.
Just close your eyes and open your heart
and feel your worries and cares depart.
Just yield yourself to the father above
and let him hold us secure in his love.
For life on earth grows more involved
with endless problems that can't be solved;
God only asks us to do our best
then he'll take over and finish the rest.
So, when you're tired, discouraged, and blue
there's always one door that's open to you and
That is the door to the house of prayer
and you will find God waiting to meet you there.
The house of prayer is no further away
than the quiet spot where you kneel and pray.
For the heart is a temple when God is there

as we place ourselves in his loving care.
And he hears every prayer and answers each one
when we pray in his name, thy will be done.
And the burden that seems too heavy to bear
are lifted away on the wings of prayer.
So, nurses you play a great part
so, keep on smiling, because God knows the heart

"And whatever things you ask in prayer, believing, you will receive."
(Matthew 21:22)

All About Carolyn

Carolyn was born on December 10, 1945.

As a young girl growing up in the fifties, she had lots of things to do. She played with her doll, "Little Raggedy Ann," made mud cakes and dishes out of clay and other goods for her playhouse.

She loved going fishing and playing with tadpoles in the branch. Carolyn would swing on grapevines to get across the branch to bigger waterholes. She didn't mind getting muddy or wet; that was her way of getting out of work. Whatever the boys did for fun, Carolyn did also.

Carolyn enjoyed going to school and she had lots of friends. She had a special friend named Daniel Raggdall, but Stephen was her heart. She cherished everything he said and did.

Stephen and Carolyn saw eye-to-eye in togetherness, and things changed for them both, for the better, when they united as one and started a family. Carolyn has three sons: Stephen Jr., Darryl, and Eric.

Carolyn attended Douglass Elementary School and Frederick Douglass Senior High School in Croom, Maryland, where she graduated in 1965.

Carolyn started attending then joined the Deliverance Church of Christ in the 1980s. She received Christ as lord and savior in 1985 where she became a member under the leadership of Bishop Robert J. Patton. Carolyn also became a member of the adult choir.

Now, under the leadership of Bishop Bobby G. Holmes and First Lady Executive Pastor, Dorothy M. Holmes, Carolyn is presently a member of the welcoming committee at Deliverance Church of Christ.

Carolyn loves to write poetry and has a great love for children and senior citizens. Her hobbies are bowling, sewing, fishing, and writing poetry.

She has six grandchildren, seven brothers (four deceased), and four sisters.

Carolyn praises God for all he has done in her life daily and for giving her the opportunity to be a witness for him, because he deserves all the glory, all the honor, and all the praise.

Printed in the United States
By Bookmasters